GW00382188

mark my words

By and Large, The Most Annoying Clichés Ever

BETTY KIRKPATRICK

Crombie Jardine
PUBLISHING LIMITED

Office 2, 3 Edgar Buildings
George Street
Bath
BA1 2FJ
www.crombiejardine.com

Published by Crombie Jardine Publishing Limited
First edition, 2008
Copyright © Crombie Jardine Publishing Limited, 2008

ISBN: 978-1-906051-20-4

Written by Betty Kirkpatrick

Cover and text designed by www.glensaville.com

Printed in China

Introduction

The word cliché is derived from the French verb *clicher* meaning to stereotype. Originally, a cliché was a printing term, a word or phrase that had been repeated time and time again in the same form from a single printing plate. 'Cliché' then became a linguistic term and this idea of something that is used again and again is at the centre of its meaning.

Cliché is often defined in dictionaries as an expression or idea that has been used so often that it is no longer effective or interesting, or words to that effect. This is the sad thing about some clichés. They were once fresh and effective ways of expressing an idea and it is ironic that these attractive features made them so overused that they became stale and sometimes annoying.

This is as true of modern expressions as it is of longer established ones. In these days of swift and global communication, changes to the language occur and spread far more quickly than they ever did before. Thus, an expression that sounds effective and interesting may become overused so quickly, especially in the media, that it becomes a cliché within a surprisingly short time. Such expressions include **between a rock and a hard place**, **flavour of the month**, **go the extra mile**, **hit the ground running**, **it goes with the territory** and **push the envelope**.

As well as these modern phrases that have become clichés quite recently, there are a great many well-established sayings that have been clichés for quite some time. There are so many of these that it was not possible to include them all in such a small book. All reference books present a challenge as what to include and what not to include and small ones obviously present even more of a challenge. This accounts for the absence of such old established idioms/clichés as **beat about the bush**, **kill two birds with one stone**, **leave no stone unturned**, **put your shoulder to the wheel** and so on.

Of course, there are many clichés that are not idioms. Many of them are simply phrases that have become overused. Some of these are long-established fixed phrases which people use without thinking, even when these are more formal, or even more archaic, than the occasion seems to demand. They include **bow to the inevitable**, **by the same token**, **a daunting prospect**, **dulcet tones**, **a moot point**, **pale into insignificance**, **the ravages of time** and **speculation is rife**.

Some circumstances attract more clichés than others. One of these, undoubtedly, involves someone who has experienced an unhappy or unfortunate event. This situation is a positive magnet for clichés, most of them extremely unhelpful, including **it's not the end of the world**, **find closure**, **just one of those things**, **pull yourself together**, **put the past behind you**, **that's life** and **these things happen**. Such clichés tend to annoy or upset people rather than bring any comfort to them.

Some clichés are particularly associated with a specific field of activity, although they may not be restricted to it. For example, the field of politics has attracted **a categorical denial**, **charm offensive**, **consider your position**, **fall on your sword**, **not fit for purpose** and **spend more time with the family**.

Other clichés are particular favourites with journalists, often tabloid journalists. These include **an accident waiting to happen**, **beleaguered**, **blazing inferno**, **the envy of the world**, **a feeding frenzy**, **grind to a halt**, **the jury's still out** and **swingeing cuts**. On the sports pages or in sports commentaries you are likely to find references to **a game of two halves** and **get a result**.

Clichés have established themselves as an essential part of our language. However, there is no doubt that people find some of them very annoying and, like so many other things, this dislike varies with personal taste. Many people particularly dislike clichés associated with the world of sales, such as **courtesy call**, **valued customer** and **your call is important to us**.

Other clichés that seem to annoy people most are those that add little or nothing to the meaning of what is said, but simply act as fillers. These include **after all is said and done**, **by and large**, **I know for a fact**, **in all honesty**, **in point of fact**, **it goes without saying**, **it's not for me to say**, **last, but not least**, **mark my words**, **needless to say**, **the thing is**, **with all due respect** and **you know what I mean**. People tend to become addicted to such clichés, often being completely unaware of how often they use them.

Some clichés are universally disliked, two of the most unpopular being **at the end of the day** and **at this moment in time**. However, we should all be careful about condemning people who use these clichés because it is all too easy to use such a cliché ourselves while we are frantically thinking of something to say in response to a formal question. Sometimes, to our embarrassment, clichés slip unbidden from our lips.

This small book contains a wide range of clichés to give readers a flavour of them, but makes no claim to be in any way comprehensive. Apologies to anyone whose most annoying cliché is not featured.

Betty Kirkpatrick
2008

The Most Annoying Clichés Ever

A

absence makes the heart grow fonder

A cliché often used in an effort to cheer up someone who is involved in a long-distance relationship. The person in receipt of this cliché often finds it annoying, especially because they are likely to hear it several times from different people and get thoroughly sick of it. Besides, there is usually someone on hand to counter this well-meaning cliché with the cynical one **out of sight, out of mind** and it is this sentiment that worries the person in a long-distance relationship. The expression **absence makes the heart grow fonder** was originally the first line of an anonymous poem published at the beginning of the seventeenth century and later became a popular saying.

accident *see* **a chapter of accidents** *(p.25)*

an accident waiting to happen

A cliché that is used, especially by journalists and other commentators, after the occurrence of almost any accident or tragedy. It points to the fact that the situation was potentially dangerous and might have resulted in tragedy at any time. However, telling those who have suffered in some way as a result of the accident or tragedy that it might have been avoided is likely to make them just feel worse.

accidents will/do happen

A cliché often said with the intention of comforting someone who has just experienced some kind of accident, whether they have caused the accident themselves or been the victim of one. The cliché stresses that accidents are an inevitable part of life, but platitudes like this often only serve to annoy or upset people who have been distressed or inconvenienced by an accident. Then there is the fact that the cliché is not necessarily true. By no means are all accidents inevitable. For example, many road accidents could be avoided if people drove more carefully, did not exceed the speed limit, did not use mobile phones while driving and so forth.

actually

A cliché that is widely used in a meaningless way by people for whom it has become an annoying habit, as in *Actually, I might just stay in tonight.* Their speech is sprinkled with the word, although they are very likely unaware of it. The word **actually** is sometimes used to add some meaning to a sentence, for example to point to the truth of something that might seem surprising or incredible, as in *I was expecting to be bored by the talk, but, actually, I found it very interesting.*

after all is said and done *same as* when all is said and done *(p.135)*

after due consideration

A cliché normally found in business letters assuring the recipient that much thought has gone into the matter. Many people find it annoying because it sounds so pompous. Also, there is often an underlying suspicion that the cliché is being used just as a polite convention and that very *little* thought has gone into the matter. As communication in general has become less formal over the years this cliché has, fortunately, gone out of fashion somewhat as has the even more formal **after earnest consideration**.

agenda *see* **hidden agenda** *(p.53)*

as a matter of fact

A cliché which is sometimes used to introduce a piece of information that will add to or emphasize what has been said already, as in *Jane is perfectly trustworthy. As a matter of fact, she regularly looks after my sister's children and Ann is very satisfied with her.* More annoyingly, the cliché is also used rather meaninglessly as a filler by people for whom it has become a habit, as in *As a matter of fact, I'm going on holiday next week.*

as I was saying

A cliché that is sometimes used to try to get back to the subject being talked about before there was some kind of interruption, as in *As I was saying before Peter came in, I think we all need to think very carefully about this before coming to a decision.* However, for some people the cliché has become just an annoying habit and it is used meaninglessly as a filler without any interruption having taken place.

asking for it

A cliché often used offensively to suggest that a woman, because of the way she was dressed or was behaving, has brought on herself, and even deserved, some sort of sexual attack, as in *The friend of the youth who's accused of raping the girl said she was wearing a very short skirt and skimpy top and was obviously asking for it.* The expression does not always have sexual overtones and can refer to any form of trouble, as in *I'm not surprised he was mugged there. He was asking for it by ignoring all our advice that it was a dangerous area at night.* When the expression is more general it has the alternative form **asking for trouble**, as in *It's asking for trouble to walk around that area at night on your own.*

at the end of the day

This is easily one of the most disliked clichés. Yet, it is widely used and often found coming from the mouths of the very people who claim to hate it. This is because it is a helpful filler cliché, used to play for time when you are thinking of something to say, for example when being asked a question on television or radio. In such situations people often use it without realizing it. This cliché is also used by people who think, quite wrongly, that it makes what they are saying sound more impressive. It is used in much the same way as **when all is said and done**.

at this moment in time

A cliché which irritates a great many people. Apart from anything else, you don't need both **moment** and **time** to convey the meaning. **At this moment** and **at this time** can stand on their own, although they are a bit pompous, and what's wrong with the simple **just now**? Yet, as is the case with **at the end of the day**, people who profess to hate it sometimes find themselves using it without intending to, as a filler cliché for something to say. The phrase is also used by people who mistakenly believe that such pompous phrases make what they are saying sound more important. **At this moment in time** became popular in America in the 1970s at the time of the investigation into Watergate, the political scandal that led to the resignation of President Richard Nixon. It crossed the Atlantic and, sadly, has never gone away.

auspicious *see* **on this auspicious occasion** *(p.95)*

avoid like the plague

An old expression that is still used as a cliché meaning to keep well away from someone or something, the plague having been particularly contagious. It has long been recognized as a cliché and appears to have annoyed several newspaper editors over the years, in the days when people worried more about sloppy English than they do now. At least I have heard several older journalists say that their editor regarded it with particular dislike, and even tried to ban it from the pages of the newspaper.

award-winning

An annoying cliché much used in promotional activities
to advertise things, such as books, theatrical performances
etc and to promote people such as authors and actors. The
cliché is meant to sound impressive but if the person or thing
that is so described has ever won an award, it is frequently
a minor, little-known one, unfamiliar to most people. Thus
a restaurant advertising itself as 'award-winning' may have
received a minor award in a small local paper and, even then,
the award might have been given quite a few years ago. *See*
highly acclaimed *(p.54).*

B

basically

A cliché that is widely used in a meaningless way by people for whom it has become an annoying habit, as in *Basically, I can't stand boiled eggs*. Although they are probably unaware of the fact, those who use this cliché often do so liberally, much to the irritation of their listeners. The word **basically** means literally or fundamentally and is sometimes used in this way, as in *The theory behind the research was basically flawed and so the findings are not valid*.

beleaguered

Not a cliché that is on everyone's lips and yet it can be very annoying, especially if you are a regular reader of newspapers, notably the tabloids. Many tabloid journalists automatically turn to this word to refer to any so-called celebrity who is in an unfortunate situation that is difficult to get out of, as in *The beleaguered pop star left the hotel by the rear entrance to avoid the paparazzi.* The word, which dates from the late sixteenth century, has come down in the world as it was originally used of a building, such as a castle or fort, or an army that was under siege.

the best possible place

A cliché frequently uttered to those lying injured in a hospital ward. Obviously, these words are intended to make the invalid feel better, that they are getting the best possible treatment. Alas, with the decline of the health service and the increase in antibiotic-resistant infections picked up in hospitals, the cliché is usually no longer apt. A better piece of advice now might be '*Get out of here as soon as possible!*'

best practice

A modern business expression used to describe a method or process that is the most effective and efficient in achieving the desired result. It sounds admirable but, unfortunately, it is one of those buzz expressions that a great many people like the sound of and overuse, whether the context is appropriate or not. Thus, it has gone from being a useful phrase to an annoying cliché in a very short time, as in *We operate a policy of best practice in all the branches of our firm.*

best-selling

A well-worn phrase applied to books or authors often as part of a publicity campaign. The idea behind the claim is, of course, to get potential buyers to think that the book has been bought by a great many people nationwide so that they too will buy it. This is by no means always the case. If there is any truth in the claim it is often restricted to a small geographical area, to a number of people in a particular field, bookshop etc. Do not assume that such a book is one of the nation's top-ten favourites.

the best thing since sliced bread *see* **the greatest thing since sliced bread** *(p.50)*

the best things in life are free

A cliché guaranteed to annoy people who are not very well-off and who know only too well that many things that would help to make their lives better are not free. The expression has its origins in the song of the title (1927) which was featured in the Broadway musical *Good News*.

better half

An expression used by some men to refer to their wives or other men's wives, as in *Hello, Mary! I don't believe you've met Jane, Jack's better half.* The expression is surprisingly old, dating from the sixteenth century. Although the phrase seems to represent a compliment, women were for a very long time by no means the better half in terms of status and, indeed, did not even have equal status in a relationship until recently. It is considered patronizing by many modern women.

between a rock and a hard place

A phrase that sounds interesting and effective the first time you hear it, but can easily become a source of irritation by the time you have heard it overused several times. A rock and a hard place in this context mean the same thing and so to be **between a rock and a hard place** means to face two equally unpleasant choices, as in *Their son's between a rock and a hard place. He's been offered a place at the university* *of his choice, but he has to start on the course right away and he's set his heart on spending a gap year working overseas.* The cliché often takes the form of **be caught between a rock and a hard place**.

bits *see* **naughty bits** *(p.88)*

blazing inferno

A cliché often found in newspapers, particularly in tabloid headlines, frequently being an exaggerated description of the extent of the fire being reported. Nothing sells newspapers like tragedy!

the bottom line

A term that has become so overused that it is in danger of becoming meaningless. As it is, it is easy to become confused with this cliché as it has more than one meaning. It can mean the most important point or factor of a situation as in *The bottom line is that we cannot afford to move house.* It can also refer to the final outcome or result of something, as in *There has been much discussion about overcrowding in schools and several proposals put forward, but the bottom line is that nothing has been done.* Originally **bottom line** was a technical term in accountancy, indicating the bottom line of a financial statement and therefore the amount of profit or loss, but it moved into the general language and became extremely popular and much overused in the 1980s.

bow to the inevitable

A cliché which sounds rather formal and literary for use in everyday speech. Nevertheless, it is quite commonly used, having become a fixed phrase indicating that something, however unpleasant or unsatisfactory, has to be accepted or tolerated, as in *We hate the idea of closing the shop, but we must bow to the inevitable. Our business has been very badly affected by the opening of the new supermarket and we're losing money.*

bread *see* **the greatest thing since sliced bread** *(p.50)*

business is business

A phrase which sums up the modern preoccupation with

money and profit. The expression is used to indicate that business takes precedence over other considerations, as in *I know you're my cousin and I'd like to be able to offer you a special discount on the car, but business is business. My company needs to make a profit.*

by and large

A cliché whose meaning is impossible to deduce from the actual wording. It is used to mean that something is mostly true, as in *By and large, the team played well.* However, it is often just used as a filler, out of habit. The cliché has a surprising origin. It was first a nautical phrase popular in the seventeenth century in the days of square-rigged ships. To sail 'by and large' meant to keep a ship on the right course and sailing at a reasonable speed, despite any change in the wind direction. It acquired its more general meaning in the eighteenth century and has survived until now as a cliché, although it is less common now than it once was.

by the same token

One of those clichés whose use is difficult to deduce from

the actual wording. It can mean *in the same way* or *for similar reasons*, as in *The new rules forbid pupils from leaving the school grounds during the school day. This restriction of their freedom has annoyed many of the pupils but, by the same token, has pleased many of the parents.* However, this is one of those annoying clichés that are often used rather uselessly by people for whom they have become a habit. The people concerned are often unaware that they use the expression so often.

a categorical denial

A statement which seems to emphasize just how strongly someone is denying something. Unfortunately, this expression is apt to arouse suspicion in those who hear it. Their instinct is to believe that the user of the cliché may be protesting their innocence too vehemently and may have something to hide, as in *The politician has issued a categorical denial that he has been having an affair with a research assistant in his department.* This is perfectly understandable as it is not unknown for, say, a politician to issue a 'categorical denial' about some misdemeanour, only to admit to the misdemeanour once members of the press have done some more investigating…

chance would be a fine thing

Quite an old cliché used when people are referring regretfully to something they would very much like to have or to experience, but are extremely unlikely to do so, as in *I'd love to go and visit Jane while she's in Australia, but chance would be a fine thing! I couldn't possibly afford the fare.*

change the goalposts *see* **move the goalposts** *(p.87)*

a chapter of accidents

A cliché used to refer to a series of misfortunes or unforeseen happenings, as in *Our journey was a chapter of accidents from beginning to end. First of all the taxi taking us to the airport was late. Then the flight was delayed for two hours. Then our luggage got mislaid and we didn't get it till two days later.*

a charm offensive

A popular phrase used to describe a sustained effort to be very pleasant and obliging to people in order to impress them. The expression was used in the mid 1980s to refer to the actions of Mikhail Gorbachev, the Soviet leader, when he was trying to make friendly overtures towards the West. It then became a more generally used cliché, popular when referring to politicians, as in *There's a general election coming up soon and our local MP will be going on a charm offensive to try to get re-elected*. Politicians rarely enjoy a very good press and anything to do with them is likely to be suspect. This is true of **a charm offensive** which is thought of as being smarmy and insincere.

children of all ages

A cliché used in a similar way to **the young of all ages**, but even more patronizing and irritating to older people.

circumstances *see* due to circumstances beyond our control *(p.34)*

find/have/get closure

A modern expression that indicates that an unpleasant or distressing event or situation has come to an end and should be forgotten about or put to the back of your mind so that you can concentrate on the future. The term has its origins in psychology, but it is now much over-used in the general language by people who are fond of giving advice to those who have suffered misfortune or distress, as in *Your husband has gone and he's not coming back. You must think of the children and seek a way to find closure.* The person at the receiving end of the cliché often finds it annoying or upsetting. People who overuse the expression doubtless think that it sounds impressive. Others think that it sounds like mumbo-jumbo.

to coin a phrase

A cliché which usually does not mean what it says. It sounds as though it should be an introduction to a phrase that has just been invented, but it is usually used to introduce a well-worn cliché. It is often used humorously or ironically, the user being perfectly aware that the phrase is far from new or innovative, as in *It's the end of an era, to coin a phrase. They've just closed down our old neighbourhood pub.*

comfort zone *see* outside your comfort zone *(p.97)*

consider your position

One of several annoying euphemistic clichés that are often used in connection with people in power, such as politicians.

It simply means that such a person is giving serious thought to whether they will have to resign or whether they will be able to get away with a misdemeanour which they may have committed, as in *The MP who revealed the confidential data to a tabloid journalist is considering his position.*

courtesy call

A term which arouses great indignation, as indeed do the telephone calls to which the term refers. Although the people who make such calls often do their best to be as polite as possible, as befits people who are on some kind of commission, a courtesy call has much more to do with inconvenience than with courtesy. A courtesy call, which, of course, is a euphemism for a sales call, however much the caller protests to the contrary, usually coincides with the times that people are at home cooking, eating, bathing or engaged in other home-based activities from which they do not wish to be disturbed. No wonder so many people now rely on their answering machines, even when they are at home. It saves them from unwelcome courtesy calls!

cradle *see* **from the cradle to grave** *(p.45)*

credit crunch

A modern cliché which became popular in international financial and economic circles in the last decades of the twentieth century and which has made its way fairly quickly into the general language. The phrase is used to refer to an economic situation in which there is a decline in the supply of credit, making it difficult for companies and individuals to borrow money, as in *Because of the credit crunch it is going to become more and more difficult for first-time buyers in the property market to get a mortgage.* The cliché became known to the general public in the UK because of worries over international banking business in America and how it would affect small private investors and borrowers in the UK. It is one of those annoying slick clichés that you feel masks the seriousness of the situation.

czar

Originally an emperor, specifically the ruler of Russia until the revolution of 1917. In the later part of the twentieth century the word began to be applied by the government to someone in charge in a particular field, as in a *drugs czar* and all too soon became a tiresome cliché. Alternative spellings include **tzar** and **tsar**.

D

a daunting prospect

A cliché which sounds rather formal or literary, but it is quite commonly used because it has become a fixed phrase and people tend not to think about the individual words. The cliché is used to indicate something difficult that you have to face that will no doubt make you nervous, as in *Moving to the large bustling city headquarters was a daunting prospect for someone who was used to the small local branch of the firm.*

day *see* **in this day and age** *(p.64)*

D-day

A cliché used to refer to a day when something is scheduled to take place or begin. Given the historical importance of the original **D-day**, the expression should be associated with something important, as in *The new cruise ship is to be launched shortly, but D-day has yet to be announced.* However, it is frequently used with reference to something relatively trivial, as in *I'm going to start a fitness class. D-day is next Monday.* Historically, D-day refers to June 6, 1944, the day in World War II on which the Allies landed on the beaches of northern France to prevent the advance of the German army. The **D** stands for the day (as the H stands for the hour in military situations: D-Day, H-Hour), although it is popularly taken to mean designated or deliverance.

dead in the water

A popular expression used, particularly in the business world, to refer to someone or something that has no chance of success, as in *The firm was doing quite well until it was hit by the recession. Now it's dead in the water.* People got very weary of the cliché in the 1980s when it was at the height of its popularity and although it is still popular, it is not quite so overused. In origin the expression refers to a fish that is dead in the water, and so of no use to a fisherman or angler.

a defining moment

A cliché which annoys people not only because it is overused but because it is more often than not used of relatively trivial events. On such occasions the user might be trying to sound impressive, but more often than not they just sound pompous. The phrase should be used to indicate an important point in the course of something, as in *That battle was to prove a defining moment in the war.*

denial *see* **a categorical denial** *(p.24)*

don't even go there!

A modern cliché which is used in informal contexts to advise someone not to talk, or go on talking, about something because it is too dreadful, distressing, embarrassing etc, as in *'What if we miss our flight?' 'Don't even go there!'*

don't hold your breath

A modern expression used to indicate that something is unlikely to happen soon or to warn someone that something might not happen until much later than they think, if ever, as in *I know that Jack promised to fix your roof this week, but don't hold your breath! Jack's not very reliable and he's very busy just now.* In origin it refers to the fact that you cannot hold your breath for very long.

due to circumstances beyond our control

A cliché acting as a standard excuse and offered as part of an apology for something being delayed, cancelled, faulty etc, as in *We apologize for any inconvenience caused to passengers by the late arrival of the train from London. This was due to circumstances beyond our control.* This cliché tends to annoy people rather than placate them as it offers no specific reason for what has gone wrong, leading to the suspicion that the phrase is just a cover-up. The cliché is no longer quite as common as it once was because companies supposedly apologizing for things going wrong, perhaps realizing that the public has got tired of the standard excuse, have become more inventive. Thus, a railway company has more than once suggested that delayed trains were a result of 'leaves on the line'. *See* **a slight technical hitch** *(p.112).*

dulcet tones

A long-standing cliché which sounds very literary for use in everyday speech, dulcet meaning sweet or melodious.

However, it is still in fairly common use today as a fixed phrase, although it is now more often used ironically, as in *We heard the dulcet tones of the pub landlady yelling 'Last orders, please!' and knew it was nearly closing time.*

E

each and every one of

A cliché mostly used as rather a pompous, repetitive way of saying **all of**. Occasionally, it is used for emphasis, as in *Each and every one of us has a duty to help to preserve the planet.*

the elephant in the room

A modern saying used to refer to a major problem that is never referred to by the people involved although it has a great effect on their lives. The expression came to be associated with the problems of alcoholism and drug-taking, but is also used more generally, as in *The marriage never really worked after Tom had an affair with his secretary. Jane tried to forget about it but it was the elephant in the room and they have now separated.*

end

see **at the end of the day** *(p.13)*

see **it'll end in tears** *(p.66)*
see **it's not the end of the world** *(p.69)*

end of

A cliché which is in line with a recent trend to use short forms of phrases that are already quite short, a trend that many older people find annoying and sloppy. It is short for **end of story**, a phrase indicating that the speaker thinks there is no more to be said on the subject, as in *We got tired of each other. We decided to part. End of.* It seems unnecessary to shorten a phrase that is already short and the result sounds abrupt and rather rude.

the end of an era

A cliché which causes annoyance because it is so often used to refer to trivial events which have lasted a relatively short time. In technical terms, an era refers to a major division of geological time. More generally, it is used of an important period of history or span of time characterized by a particular feature, event, person etc, such as *the Tudor era in English history.* In both cases, the word era suggests importance and great length of time. It is, thus, fine to refer to the death of Queen Victoria or to the demise of the last steam train line as the **end of an era**. However, an event such as the moving away of your next-door neighbours after five years or so, is not the end of an era.

the envy of the world

A cliché used to emphasize how much better something is somewhere, usually Britain, than elsewhere, as in *We must not forget the fact that our health service is the envy of the world.* The cliché has become very annoying because, most of the time, it is no longer true, if it ever was. The expression is sometimes used by journalists who are appealing to our patriotism, but mostly by politicians who are trying to convince us that they are doing a splendid job of running the country so that life here is better than anywhere else.

every effort is being made *see* explore every avenue

explore every avenue

An over-used phrase which people find annoying often

because they believe that the user is either not telling the truth or is greatly exaggerating. Frequently found in rather formal contexts, the expression is used to indicate that someone is trying very hard to investigate something thoroughly and to find a solution to it, as in *We have not yet found your missing documents, but you have our assurance that we are exploring every avenue in our efforts to locate them.* However, the person being given this assurance often regards it as a euphemism for doing very little. The word 'avenue' here means approach or means of access and may have a military origin. An alternative, and less formal, version of this cliché is **every effort is being made**.

extra *see* **go the extra mile** *(p.49)*

F

fact

see **as a matter of fact** *(p.11)*

see **in point of fact** *(p.63)*

fall on your sword

This phrase annoys people because it somehow suggests a heroism that is often singularly absent from the situation which it is used to describe. The modern cliché is often used to refer to the action of someone, often in political or business circles, who has resigned from a position of power or importance. The resignation usually arises from some misdemeanour they have been found committing and often occurs just before they were going to be sacked anyhow, as in *The prime minister would have had no choice but to ask for the minister's resignation in the light of his scandalous behaviour, but the minister decided to fall on his sword.* Heroism usually does not come into it. Historically, falling on their swords was a method of suicide favoured by Roman generals after a military defeat and is more obviously heroic. The phrase is biblical in origin.

far be it from me to…

One of those annoying clichés that suggest that someone is not going to make any comment, although it is, in fact, only an introduction to what they *are* going to say, as in *Far be it from me to tell her how to lead her life, but I really wouldn't advise her to marry him.* The cliché seems to indicate that the person does not feel qualified or suited to comment on a situation, but the phrase is often used meaninglessly, having become a habit with the person concerned. They use it to introduce a whole range of comments, however irrelevant. The expression, which is a very old one, dating from the fourteenth century, can sound rather formal and pompous.

a feeding frenzy

A cliché that is often used to describe a pack of news-hungry journalists or press photographers who rush frantically forward to surround the source of the news item, as in *As soon as it was announced that Princess Di was to attend the event, international journalists flew in immediately and indulged in their usual feeding frenzy.* The cliché sounds unpleasant because of its associations. The expression is used to refer to the behaviour of sharks when they move in wildly and aggressively to get their share of a prey that one of their group has attacked.

festive season

A term which many people find annoying as a way of referring to the period around Christmas, perhaps regretting the fact that it makes no actual mention of Christmas and so ignores the Christian element of the festival. The useful thing about the expression is that it is a succinct way of describing the whole of the holiday period around Christmas and New Year, a holiday period which seems to get longer every year.

final analysis *see* **in the final analysis** *(p.64)*

find/have/get closure *see* **closure** *(p.26)*

flavour of the month

A cliché which, like many others, sounds interesting and effective the first few times you hear it, but becomes tedious when it is over overused, as this one often is. The cliché is used to describe something or someone that is extremely popular for a short period of time, as in *Jack never stays with the same girlfriend for long. Just now Sue's the flavour of the month, but that'll soon change.* The expression has its origin in advertising, being a phrase used in America (where 'flavour' becomes 'flavor') to try to get customers to extend the range of ice cream flavours they enjoyed by introducing a different special flavour each month.

a fond farewell

A cliché that is supposed to suggest that you are saying farewell, often permanently, to someone or something that you are fond of, as in *Close friends joined his widow and family in the country churchyard to say a fond farewell to this famous entertainer.* However, the expression is often used to mean to say a final goodbye to someone or something, irrespective of whether you are fond of them, are completely indifferent to them or heartily dislike them. This use is particularly common in journalese.

frankly *see* **quite frankly** *(p.105)*

-friendly *see* **user-friendly** *(p.129)*

friendly fire

A phrase that is really a military euphemism for gunfire or bombs that kill or injure people who are on the same side as the person responsible for the attack. Obviously, such attacks are usually the result of an accident, error or carelessness, rather than a deliberate attempt to kill an ally, but calling the attack **friendly fire** is highly inappropriate and, indeed, grotesque. Certainly the relatives of anyone killed in this way will not regard the gunfire as friendly.

… from hell

A cliché used to describe someone or something that is the worst possible, as in She *was the flatmate from hell!* and *It was the train journey from hell.* The expression leapt to popularity in the 1990s and is still very common, especially in tabloid headlines. Bad neighbours, in particular, are frequently described in the tabloids as being from hell.

from the cradle to the grave

An expression which is used to mean a person's life from birth to death. In the twentieth century the expression became a cliché associated with the philosophy of the welfare state, as in *Many of us think that the National Health Service has a duty to look after us from the cradle to the grave.* Whether you find it particularly annoying or not can depend on your political affiliation. Although the expression emerged as a political cliché relatively recently, it has been in the language for much longer. It is thought to have been coined by essayist Sir Richard Steele in the early eighteenth century. Winston Churchill used the expression in a radio broadcast in 1943: *'National compulsory insurance for all classes for all purposes from the cradle to the grave'.*

G

gambit *see* **opening gambit** *(p.95)*

a game of two halves

A cliché much used by football commentators and likely to annoy those who are not avid football fans who happen to tune into such a commentary. It seems unnecessary to remind us that a football match has two halves, but commentators often use it to underline the fact that the outcome of the match cannot be predicted by the first half and both luck and standard of play can change in the second half, as in *There's no doubt that they were the better team in the first half, but they're showing signs of tiring, and it's a game of two halves, after all.* There is not always something interesting happening in a football match and commentators find this cliché comes in handy as a space filler. From time to time the cliché shows signs of becoming more generally used.

game plan

An irritating cliché which refers to a strategy worked out in advance in order to achieve an objective. Annoyingly, it is often used rather grandly or pompously when the simple word **plan** would suffice, as in *This is our game plan for our holiday. We'll take the plane to Paris, spend a few days there and then hire a car to drive to Nice which we'll use as a base.* The expression is derived from an American football term.

get a life

A modern remark used rather rudely to suggest that the person addressed leads an uninteresting and restricted life and needs to extend their range of interests and experience, and perhaps learn to accept things, as in *There's nothing wrong with the child having a mobile. All the kids have them these days. Get a life!*

get a result

A cliché which many people find annoying because they regard the word **result** as having only its original meaning of outcome or consequence and capable of being either good or bad, depending on the circumstances. The modern cliché **get a result**, which began in the world of football, however, means to achieve a favourable outcome, as in *The team must get a result this week to stay at the top of the league.* It then became more generally used. For example, the police sometimes use the expression to mean to succeed in arresting someone for a crime.

get into trouble

An old cliché used as a euphemism to refer to a woman getting pregnant while she is unmarried. The expression gives the impression, unfairly and, of course, quite wrongly, that the woman has got into this situation all by herself and this impression is reinforced by the alternative form of the cliché **get herself into trouble**. Fortunately, this cliché is now rather old-fashioned as it is no longer generally considered a disgrace for a woman to have a child while unmarried.

get out of bed on the wrong side

A cliché used to refer to someone who is in an exceptionally cross mood, as in *Tom's in a foul mood this morning. He must have got out of bed on the wrong side.* If you are already in a bad mood someone applying this cliché to you is likely to make you feel even more annoyed. The expression is probably linked to the fact that it was once considered unlucky to put your left foot on the ground first when getting out of bed.

go the extra mile

One of those clichés that can sound interesting and effective until you hear it so often that you find it annoying. It means to put in the extra amount of effort, money etc that will allow the achievement of something, as in *The council have already done a great deal to help homeless people, but they need to go the extra mile and provide the funding for hostels and other budget accommodation.* The expression began to be exceptionally popular in the late twentieth century, although it was around before that, at least earlier in the twentieth century. It has been suggested that the expression has its origin in the Bible where Jesus in Matthew 5:41 says *And whosoever compel thee to go a mile, go with him two.* Although the wording is not the same, the sentiment is similar.

grave *see* **have one foot in the grave** *(p.52)*

the greatest thing since sliced bread

A cliché used to refer to someone or something exceptionally good or marvellous, as in *My mother thinks her new kitchen gadget is the greatest thing since sliced bread*. This cliché might well puzzle younger people who might, justifiably, not understand why sliced bread is seen as such a great thing. There have been a great many inventions in recent decades, such as television and computers, which have had much more of an impact on human life than sliced bread. Pre-sliced bread first appeared on shop shelves in the 1920s, but the date of the expression based on it is uncertain. Nowadays, many people prefer to buy their bread unsliced, thus causing even more confusion to those trying to understand the expression. The cliché is often used to refer to people who have an over-inflated opinion of themselves, as in *The new member of the team isn't very good, but he thinks he's the greatest thing since sliced bread*. An alternative form of the expression is **the best thing since sliced bread**.

grind to a halt

A favourite cliché amongst journalists. Every time something comes to a stop there is a good possibility that you will read that it has ground to a halt, as in *Talks have ground to a halt once again.* The phrase probably originates in the grinding noise made by a train when it comes to an emergency stop.

ground-breaking

A cliché which supposedly means pioneering or innovative, referring to significant new discoveries, developments or methods, as in *His ground-breaking research led to a new range of drugs for the treatment of heart disease.* Unfortunately, it is often overused and used to refer, inappropriately, to something that is neither especially innovative nor especially significant, as in *her ground-breaking additions to romantic fiction.* The cliché is from the idiom **break new ground** which has its origins in the fact that the ground is broken at the start of a building operation.

H

happen

> *see* **accidents will/do happen** *(p.9)*
> *see* **an accident waiting to happen** *(p.9)*
> *see* **these things happen** *(p.121)*

harm *see* **it never did me any harm** *(p.67)*

have a nice day!

A greeting used, for example, by shop assistants to customers as they leave the shop. It was first used in America and is much more commonly used and accepted there than in the UK. In the UK many people regard it as an annoying cliché.

have one foot in the grave

An expression, dating from the sixteenth century, which, literally, indicates that someone is close to death, being either very old or very ill. As a cliché, it is often used as an insulting or disrespectful term to someone who is either elderly or considered past it by the user of the cliché, as in *Fred says that his head of department has one foot in the grave and should be given early retirement to make way for a younger man – Fred!*

a heady mixture

A cliché used to indicate a combination that is very exciting and liable to go to people's heads, as in *To her he was completely irresistible. He was that heady mixture of money, power and good looks.* It is a fixed phrase with its origin in the effect that strong alcoholic drink has on people.

hidden agenda

A cliché used to refer to someone's undisclosed motives or aims, as in *Unlike the rest of us, she is in favour of the new hotel complex, but she has a hidden agenda. Her mother-in-law owns some of the land and will make a fortune if the scheme goes ahead.* We live in an age of suspicion and this has become a very common expression to the extent that it has become irritating. The word **agenda** is sometimes used instead of the whole expression to refer to someone's underlying motives or aims, as in *He is a very devious young man and I am sure that he is supporting the scheme because of some agenda of his own.* Until recently, agenda had only a business meaning and referred to a list of things to be discussed in a formal meeting, as in *This matter is not on the agenda for the board meeting.*

hell *see* **… from hell** *(p.44)*

highly acclaimed

An annoying cliché much used in promotional activities to advertise books, theatrical performances etc. Not only is the expression overused, often it is used rather dishonestly. Things are sometimes described as highly acclaimed when they have received only the briefest of mentions in a little-known publication, or wrongly described as highly acclaimed when they are quite new on the market (too new for critics and the public to have had time to assess them!). *See* **award-winning** *(p.15)*.

a historic occasion

A tiresome cliché which causes annoyance not only because it is much overused, but because it is often used quite inappropriately of events which are of little importance. Taken literally, the phrase should be used to refer to an event that is of some historical importance, as in *It was a historic occasion when the two leaders signed the treaty that ended many years of bitter warfare.* Even when used more loosely, the expression should be reserved for an event of some great importance. Yet we frequently find it used of such occasions as the defeat of one local team by another for the first time.

hit the ground running

An expression that sounds interesting and effective the first time you hear it, but can easily become a source of irritation by the time you have heard it overused several times. The cliché refers to someone who begins some new activity with energy, enthusiasm and effectiveness right from the start and is much used in a business context, as in *New recruits to our sales team will all be expected to hit the ground running.* The expression has a military background, referring to soldiers jumping from a helicopter or getting up from landing by parachute and, without delay, running into battle or to perform the task assigned to them.

hold *see* **I'll just pop you on hold** *(p.59)*

I

icon

A word that was once used in much more restricted contexts than it is today. In the nineteenth century it was used to refer to a picture or image of a holy person in the Greek or Russian Orthodox Church. In this meaning it has the alternative spelling **ikon**. From around the later part of the twentieth century the word icon came to refer to someone or something that attracted a great deal of admiration, especially when they were regarded as symbolizing an idea, philosophy, way of life etc, as in *Marilyn Monroe was regarded as an icon of glamorous Hollywood*. It was frequently used by journalists and commentators to describe Diana, Princess of Wales. Icon became very popular and began to be used very loosely to refer to anyone or anything relatively popular or well-known and became a cliché, as in *The winner of the competition became, within a few weeks, an icon of the pop music industry*. Even more annoying than the overuse of icon is the overuse of the adjective derived from it, **iconic**. This cliché appears in such rather meaningless contexts as *an iconic range of designer furniture.*

I dare say

One of those annoying clichés that does not mean what it says. The wording suggests that the speaker is about to be bold or adventurous in what they have to say. Instead, it is simply rather a meaningless introduction to a statement, indicating what is probably true, as in *I dare say she was just trying to help him, but he thought she was interfering.* The cliché is often used as a filler by people for whom it has become a habit.

I hate to mention it but…

A tiresome cliché which is often used to introduce a remark that the person addressed is unlikely to want to hear, as it is usually a reference to a fault or problem of some kind, as in *I hate to mention it but if you spend any more time on your make-up you're going to be late.* The cliché is often used meaninglessly as a filler, having become a habit, but sometimes the speaker actually relishes bringing some bad news to someone, as in *I hate to mention it but the dress you've bought for the wedding is identical to the one the bride's mother is going to wear.*

I know for a fact…

Another annoying cliché because the **for a fact** is completely redundant. **I know** is quite sufficient on its own or you can even omit the whole phrase and simply make your comment. The cliché is sometimes used to lay particular emphasis on what is being said, but, more often, people use it as a filler out of habit and may be quite unaware that they are doing so.

I'll just pop you on hold

An extremely annoying cliché often used by the person on the other end of the line when you are in the middle of an urgent call and short of time, as in *I'll just pop you on hold while I check those details.* You know that, at the very least, you are in for a long wait and that you will be left hopping up and down with impatience with no one to vent your rage on. The cliché is all the more annoying because you have more than a sneaking suspicion that the person answering your call has put the receiver down and forgotten all about you or is just hoping that you will simply hang up, as you frequently do!

I'm just doing my job

A cliché used by people in some kind of authority, often a fairly minor position, to indicate that they are simply following the procedure as laid out by the terms of their jobs when they refuse carry out someone's request, as in *There's no point in complaining that I won't let you park here. I'm just doing my job.* Often they are being overzealous and unnecessarily inflexible and the cliché arouses great irritation in the person making the request.

I must say

One of those annoying expressions that do not mean what they say. Usually, there is no suggestion that the person using it is under any compulsion to make the statement that follows it, as in *I must say that this is a lovely garden.* Instead, it is a filler cliché which has become an annoying habit with many people.

in all conscience

One of those clichés whose meaning is difficult to deduce from the wording. It is used to mean to be fair or to do what you think is right, as in *I cannot in all conscience say that I think she is suitable for the job*, but it is often used rather meaninglessly by people for whom it has become a habit and a source of annoyance to their friends and acquaintances.

in all honesty

A cliché which sounds as though the person using it is doing so to emphasize the truth of what they are saying, as though the listener were likely to query this. This is not usually the case. The cliché is usually used meaninglessly as a filler by people for whom it has become an annoying habit, as in *In all honesty, I think we should go by bus.* See **to be honest** (p.123).

in a parlous state

An old-fashioned sounding cliché used to indicate that

something or someone is in a very bad way, as in *The economy is in a parlous state and a wage freeze for public-sector workers has just been announced*. **Parlous** here is an archaic form of perilous and, like the word, the expression is an old one. It may seem strange that it is used in everyday speech, but it has become a fixed phrase. Shakespeare used it in his play *As You Like It* (1598) – *Thou art in a parlous state, shepherd*.

inappropriate behaviour

An annoying cliché used, often euphemistically, to cover a wide range of behaviour that is considered not correct or proper, from the slightly unsuitable to the wildly indecent to the absolutely immoral to the downright illegal. It is often used by people in authority in education, social services etc. At its worst, it is a euphemism for serious abusive actions, as in *He has been accused of indulging in inappropriate behaviour with both of his daughters after his wife died*.

in a relationship

A cliché used to refer to a romantic or sexual relationship of varying degrees of length. It seems to have replaced everything from going out with someone to living with someone, as in *I was in a relationship for a few months, but we've just split up*. Those who are not romantically or sexually involved often feel it necessary to say *I'm not in a relationship at the moment*. The expression can annoy people by its very overuse.

I need some space

An annoying cliché ostensibly used to put in a plea for more personal freedom or opportunity and time to do what you want to do, but often used by people who are trying to extricate themselves from a relationship, as in *It's not that I don't love you anymore. It's just that I think we should take a break for a while. I need some space*. A cop-out!

in point of fact

A rather formal-sounding cliché. It could almost be mistaken for a legal term. Instead, it is frequently used rather meaninglessly to introduce a remark, as in *In point of fact, I have never met him*. The cliché is popular as a filler by people for whom it has become an annoying habit.

in the final analysis

A cliché sometimes used to refer to the most important points about a situation, as in *There have been bitter arguments over which of the estranged couple should have custody of the children, but, in the final analysis, the happiness and well-being of the children must come first.* Often, however, the cliché does not add anything much to the meaning of what is being said and some people use it simply as a filler cliché. This cliché tends to be used by people who think that it makes what they are saying seem more impressive. It is used in the same way as **at the end of the day** and **when all is said and done**. Earlier forms of the expression include **in the ultimate analysis** and **in the last analysis**.

in this day and age

A weary cliché used as a rather pretentious filler when a simple **now** or **nowadays** would do, as in *With all the various forms of communication around in this day and age you'd think that they could stay in touch with their parents!* Like all filler clichés it becomes an annoying habit with many people who may well be unaware of how often they use it.

issues

A modern cliché meaning problems or difficulties. Most of us are used to **issues** meaning things to be discussed and clarified, as in *The most important issues to be discussed at the meeting concern the budget for next year.* However, we are gradually being infiltrated by the rather annoying modern American use in the sense of problems, as in *We cannot take a vacation this year. My husband has health issues.*

… is the new …

A cliché dating from the 1990s which became so common that it became extremely annoying. It has been used in a wide range of contexts, as in *Purple is the new black on the catwalk this autumn* and *Style bars are the new pubs in the city's trendier areas.* It became less popular, largely because it reached saturation point, but, unfortunately, it has never completely gone away.

it goes without saying that…

One of those annoying clichés that suggest that someone is not going to make any comment, although, in fact, the cliché is only an introduction to what is going to be said. In the case of this cliché the idea is that no one need make any comment because the comment that follows the cliché is generally known or accepted, although this might not be the case, as in *It goes without saying that all workers will be given equal rights*. As is the case with many clichés, this expression has become an annoying habit with many people and they use it without thinking of the meaning. The cliché **needless to say** is used in the same way.

it goes with the territory

A cliché indicating that it is usual for a particular kind of problem or difficulty to occur in connection with a particular kind of activity or situation, as in *All teenagers rebel against their parents. It goes with the territory.* This is one of several annoying clichés used to tell people that they just have to accept a situation. In origin the expression probably refers to the territory or area covered by a particular salesman.

it'll end in tears

An expression once used a great deal by parents to warn

their children that whatever they were playing at was likely to end in someone getting hurt. Naturally, children found the phrase extremely irritating, not least because the warning was so often quite justified. Nowadays, when children are allowed so much less freedom to play in situations which might prove hurtful or dangerous, perhaps fewer parents find it necessary to issue this warning, but I am sure it remains firmly fixed in the minds of those for whom it was a daily part of childhood. The cliché has now stepped beyond the confines of childhood and is used as a more general warning of a likely unfortunate outcome, as in *They shouldn't really take out such a huge mortgage when they don't have secure jobs: it'll end in tears.*

it never did me any harm

A saying often used by older people to refer to something that happened to them that was harsh by modern standards, as in *I was given physical punishment at school and it never did me any harm.* The implication is often that modern life is too soft and young people over-indulged. Young people, especially, find the cliché annoying.

it's for your own good

A favourite with parents, this cliché is much used by those in authority to young people in a vain effort to convince them that a certain course of action, often some form of punishment, will benefit them eventually, although it will seem unpleasant or harsh now, as in *We're confiscating your mobile until you have paid off the bill with your pocket money. It's for your own good. You need to learn the value of money.* Naturally, it is a cliché which annoys young people greatly and enduring the punishment or unpleasant treatment annoys them even more. They do not see any future benefit arising from it.

it's not for me to say, but …

One of those annoying clichés that suggest that someone is not going to make any comment, although it is, in fact, only an introduction to what they *are* going to say, as in *It's not for me to say, but that young man is going to end up in prison.* The phrase is frequently used by people for whom it has become an annoying habit. They are using it meaninglessly as a filler and are often not conscious of doing so.

it's not rocket science

A phrase which is used to indicate that something is quite simple to do and does not require great brain power or technical ability, as in *Surely you can put that small table together. It's hardly rocket science and the instructions are there.* It is easy to say this if you have the necessary knowledge and understanding to perform a certain task, but people who are struggling with it find the cliché annoying. The expression is based on the assumption that those engaged in space science have exceptional minds and certainly they were much admired during the 1960s and 1970s when America's space programme was at its most successful.

it's not the end of the world

A well-meaning cliché used to try to minimize the distress that someone is experiencing by reminding them that the cause of their distress is relatively minor compared with major tragedy, as in *I know you're unhappy that Sam has left you, but it's not the end of the world.* The cliché rarely brings any comfort to the sufferer and will certainly annoy them if their misery allows them to take it in.

it stands to reason

A cliché whose wording is difficult to understand. It can be taken to mean that what is being said should be clear to any sensible person, as in *It stands to reason that organic vegetables will be a bit more expensive.* However, the expression is often used quite meaninglessly by people for whom it has become a habit and they are sometimes unaware how much they use it.

it's the thought that counts

A cliché which is often uttered as a conventional response to the giving of a gift of little monetary value, as in *My daughter gave me this little book for my 60th birthday. She's a penniless student and, anyway, it's the thought that counts.* It is often used ironically to refer to low-value gifts that are positively mean in the circumstances, as in *Our children gave us a box of chocolates on our silver wedding anniversary. Still, it's the thought that counts.*

it's time to move on

An unwelcome expression used to people who have

experienced grief or some misfortune to try to get them to forget the past and to plan for the future, as in *I know you loved your husband very much, but he wouldn't want you to spend your life grieving. It's time to move on.* The cliché rarely brings any comfort to the sufferer who may well not have the strength to contemplate the future and it can be a source of irritation, especially if several people use it. Some people feel compelled to give advice to people suffering from misfortune and this often takes the form of a cliché. *See* **put the past behind you** *(p.103).*

jaundiced *see* **look on someone or something with a jaundiced eye** *(p.79)*

the jewel in the crown

A cliché used to refer to the best or most outstanding part of anything, as in *The new young designer has produced an interesting and innovative collection and the jewel in the crown of the collection is a very chic scarlet evening dress.* The expression was popularized by the television adaptation of Paul Scott's *Raj Quartet* novels in 1984. The first of these novels was entitled *The Jewel in the Crown* (1966), the jewel being India and the crown being that of Queen Victoria. The novel gave its name to the television series. The expression was commonly used to refer to the British colonies when Britain had an empire, but it did not become a cliché until the television series popularized it. It then became annoyingly overused, particularly in journalese.

job *see* **I'm just doing my job** *(p.60)*

journey *see* **on a journey** *(p.92)*

the jury's still out

A cliché used to indicate that no decision has yet been made, as in *The jury's still out on whether they'll get planning permission for the new hotel complex, but there's a lot of local opposition to it.* Juries in the law courts have been around for a long time, but the cliché referring to them is surprisingly new, being thought to have become popular in the early 1980s. It became so liked and overused, particularly by journalists, that it became irritating.

just between you and me

An expression that sounds as though the user is about to impart something highly confidential or secret that will make for a juicy piece of gossip, and sometimes it is, indeed, used in this way, as in *Just between you and me, I hear that the new receptionist is the manager's mistress.* However, it is often used meaninglessly just as a filler by people for whom it has become an irritating habit. It is common for people to use the expression **just between you and I** under the (wrong) impression that this is grammatically correct.

just one of those things

One of several clichés which refer to the inevitability or unpredictability of some things or situations. The cliché can be very annoying to the person on the receiving end, as the fact that some things are inevitable is not a source of comfort if something unpleasant or distressing has happened to you, as in *It's a pity that your boyfriend's been transferred to London, but it's just one of those things.* The Cole Porter song of the name popularized the expression.

K

killing fields

A cliché used, often by journalists, to refer to a scene of mass killing, as in *UN representatives suspected that mass slaughter of villagers had taken place but it took them some time to identify the killing fields.* The expression was popularized by a film of the name (1984) about genocide in Cambodia, although the expression predates the film by a few years. The cliché is sometimes used to refer to exceptionally harsh treatment in general, as in *They went straight from school into the killing fields of the cotton trade and many of them died young.*

kiss and tell

A cliché used to mean to reveal intimate details about an affair, as in *The MP should have known that his young girlfriend was the type to kiss and tell.* The expression became well-known as a cliché in the 1980s when several people revealed to the tabloid press details of illicit affairs with people in power. Since the informants were usually well-paid for these details the cliché acquired the alternative form **kiss and sell**. **Kiss and tell** is a surprisingly old expression, having been known since the late seventeenth century.

know *see* **I know for a fact** *(p.59)*

know what I mean *see* **you know what I mean** *(p.139)*

know what I think? *see* **you know what I think?** *(p.139)*

L

last but not least

This cliché is frequently used when a list of names or items, in which there is no obvious order of merit, is read out, as in *Finally, last but not least, Jane White, will also be joining our marketing department*. It is an annoying expression because it is so predictable. The expression is a very old one, dating from the sixteenth century and so we have been putting up with it for a very long time.

the late-lamented

A cliché used to refer someone or something to a person or thing that is no longer around. It sounds as though the person or thing referred to is much missed and this is sometimes the case, as in *the late-lamented Martin Luther King*. Sometimes, though, the cliché is used in a humorous or ironic way to refer to someone or something that is not missed at all, as in *That is the site of the late-lamented tower block. Thankfully, it was demolished two years ago.*

learning curve

A cliché which is often used simply to refer to the fact that someone has learned or experienced something useful, as in *My son's work in Africa during his gap year is not at all relevant to his university course, but it's a useful learning curve.* This annoying cliché is often used with the intention of making a statement sound more impressive and often the user does not actually know what it means. The phrase **learning curve** originally meant the rate at which something, such as a new skill, was learned, the expression being first used to refer to a graph which plotted this rate.

let me tell you

One of those expressions which does not really mean what it seems to say; it is not asking for permission to inform someone of something. It is sometimes used to add emphasis, but it is often used as a filler by people for whom it has become a habit, as in *Let me tell you, I know what I saw.*

a level playing field

A cliché of sporting origin that indicates a situation which is completely fair to everyone involved because none of the participants has an advantage of any kind, as in *The government in power there is claiming that the forthcoming election will be a level playing field, but several international commentators disagree with this claim.* The expression infiltrated the UK from America in the 1980s and seemed to achieve overnight widespread coverage. The cliché annoys people from the extent of its overuse and perhaps from the fact that it refers to a situation which rarely exists.

life

see **get a life** *(p.47)*
see **that's life** *(p.120)*

look on someone or something with a jaundiced eye

An old-fashioned sounding cliché whose meaning is to view someone or something from a cynical or pessimistic viewpoint, as in *Most of the neighbours look at the youths who stand at the street corner with a jaundiced eye, but some of those youths do useful work with disabled children.* It is an unpleasant sounding cliché and it has an unpleasant origin, being a reference to an old, and erroneous, belief that people suffering from jaundice, a condition in which the skin and the whites of the eyes turn yellow, see everything as though it were coloured yellow.

loose cannon

An expression referring to someone who can be a liability to their friends and acquaintances because of their unpredictable and often reckless behaviour, as in *I'm a bit worried about Pete's wife coming to the office party. She's quite sensible when she's sober, but she can be a bit of a loose cannon when she's had a few drinks.* The expression was applied to Diana, Princess of Wales by people who disapproved of her and this may have helped to popularize the cliché. It is one of those expressions that you may find interesting and effective the first few times but becomes a source of annoyance when you hear it too often. In origin, the expression refers to a cannon carried by a sailing ship. The cannons had to be secured by ropes to keep them from rolling about in heavy storms as they were very heavy and might have done a great deal of damage if they were loose.

lose the plot

A cliché used in informal contexts to mean to cease to understand what is going on and to become confused, or to lose control of a situation. The expression probably has its origins in the plot of a play, book or film. The cliché can become quite unpleasant when, as frequently happens, it is used to describe someone who may be suffering from some kind of memory loss or dementia, as in *I think the old boss should retire and hand over to his son. He's beginning to lose the plot.*

loved ones

A cliché used to refer to the family and close friends of someone who has just died, has been involved in a serious accident, is seriously ill etc, as in *To add to the distress of his loved ones, the police say that it will be some time before they can release the body of the murdered man for burial.* It is impossible to say whether the cliché is a true description because no one is in a position to say which relatives and friends, if any, of someone who is either dead or unconscious were or are actually loved by them. Nevertheless the cliché has become a widespread convention.

M

make no mistake

The wording of this cliché suggests that it is a warning to someone not to commit an error or get something wrong, but, in fact, the meanings of the words are not really relevant. The cliché is sometimes used for emphasis, as in *Make no mistake. He does not deserve this treatment.* However, it is also used without thinking by people for whom it has become an annoying habit. An alternative form is **make no mistake about it**.

mark my words

This cliché sounds as though it is trying to impress the listener with the importance of what the speaker is going to say. However, it is more usually a meaningless remark that has just become an annoying habit on the part of the speaker, as in *Mark my words. The bus will be late again.*

meaningful dialogue

An annoying, pompous cliché used in political and business circles and originating in America. The expression is doubtless used to try to impress people with the importance and seriousness of the talks referred to, as in *The council have been engaged in meaningful dialogue with transport experts for some months, but no new proposals for alleviating the town's traffic problems have yet been put forward.* The cliché fails to impress most people.

merciful release

A cliché used to indicate a death that comes after a painful, and often long, illness, and so puts an end to suffering, as in *She was in agony with terminal cancer and death came as a merciful release.* Sometimes the cliché is more applicable to the relatives than the patients, although this is not stated, as in *He died last night and, having been in a coma for more than a year, his death was a merciful release.*

moment

see **at this moment in time** *(p.13)*
see **a defining moment** *(p.32)*

the moment of truth

An expression that annoys some people because, although it is a formal-sounding expression with a dramatic origin, it is so often used of extremely minor situations, as in *Dad says he's mended the chair, but the moment of truth will be when someone sits on it.* It is sometimes found in deliberately humorous contexts. The expression is a translation of the Spanish *el momento de la verdad* which refers to the point in a bullfight at which the matador is about to kill the bull.

a moot point

A cliché meaning a debatable or doubtful point. It sounds too literary and archaic to be used much in everyday language, but it is quite commonly found in all but the most informal contexts, as in *It is a moot point whether this is still the best French restaurant in the town. Recently it has begun to have some serious opposition.* Some people overuse the cliché in inappropriate situations because they do not know what the expression means. Most people using the cliché do so automatically without stopping to think of the origin, but a **moot point** was originally used to refer to something that was worthy of discussion in a **moot**. A **moot** was an Anglo-Saxon term for a meeting and from the sixteenth century it was used for a meeting of law students where points of law of particular interest were discussed.

move on *see* **it's time to move on** *(p.70)*

movers and shakers

A cliché describing people who are particularly active and innovative, as in *There are a few movers and shakers on the board, but they are outnumbered by the older, ultra-conservative directors.* There are people who dislike the cliché and who dislike the people that it describes because they themselves do not care for too much change or activity. They tend to use the cliché in a derogatory way, as in *They're bound to appoint one of those movers and shakers to the marketing post. It'll be someone who knows nothing about the product or the competition and who'll make massive changes that won't work.* The cliché only gained popularity in the last few decades, but the expression has its origins in a poem by Arthur O'Shaughnessy (1874), although the poem relates to creative people rather than business people, as in *We are the music-makers/We are the dreamers of dreams/...Yet we are the movers and shakers/Of the world forever, it seems.*

move the goalposts

A sporting cliché with its origins in football meaning to change the aims, guidelines, conditions, rules etc of a project after it is already under way, as in *We are trying to finalize the costings for the new school, but the council members keep moving the goalposts. They don't seem to know what they want.* The expression is not often used in football, but it is very much overused in the general language.

N

nanny state

A cliché used to refer to a country that is run by an over-protective government. The expression was popularized in the 1980s by supporters of Margaret Thatcher who were against the power of the Welfare State saying that it encouraged people to be too dependent on the state, as in *There are far too many people on benefit in this nanny state. We need to get more people out to work.* The expression was coined by the Conservative politician Iain MacLeod in 1965. Even after Labour came into power the cliché continued to be popular, being used to refer to undue interference by the government in people's private lives, as in *These suggested ID cards are just another example of the nanny state.*

naughty bits

A euphemism for the genitals and a rather annoying one, as it sounds unnecessarily coy and twee in this outspoken age, as in *Close the curtains while you're changing or the neighbours will see your naughty bits.* The phrase originates in a lecture on the parts of the body in *Monty Python's Flying Circus* (1970), an episode in the BBC satirical comedy series (1969-74), although it did not become a cliché until more recently. Sometimes the expression is shortened to just **bits**, as in *He'd just come out of the bath and he was wearing a towel that barely covered his bits.*

needless to say

One of those clichés that suggest that someone is not going to make any comment, although, in fact, the cliché is only an introduction to what is going to be said. In the case of this cliché, the idea is that no one need make any comment because the comment that follows the cliché is generally known or accepted, although this might not be the case, as in *Needless to say, every application for help will be treated sympathetically.* As is the case with many clichés, this expression has become an annoying habit with many people and they use it without thinking of the meaning. The cliché **it goes without saying** is used in the same way.

needs no introduction

An annoying cliché much used by people introducing someone, such as an after-dinner speaker, who is about to address a group of people. Members of the audience who appreciate brevity on such occasion should not, however, feel any relief at this statement. The person using such an opening cliché is very likely to go on to introduce the speaker at great length, as in *Our after-dinner speaker is someone who needs no introduction. He is known to all of you as one of the town's most successful businessmen. He is also known for his voluntary work, in particular his work with young people. He is…*

new *see* **… is the new …** *(p.65)*

nice *see* **have a nice day!** *(p.52)*

no pain, no gain

A cliché which many of us find annoying partly because it is often true! It is based on a nineteenth-century proverb that indicates that no advantage or benefit is ever achieved without some form of disadvantage, trouble, sacrifice etc being involved. Nowadays, it is often applied to visiting the gym, where people work very hard to achieve what they regard as the perfect body shape, or to dieting, which people undertake in order to achieve the same goal. Their aim may be loss, in the form of weight, rather than gain, but there is certainly pain.

not fit for purpose

A modern cliché that has become annoying within a very short time. It arose in political circles and is still particularly popular among politicians. It is easy to understand the politicians' liking for this cliché because it neatly avoids the necessity for saying just exactly what is wrong with something or indeed of indicating what is the exact purpose of something. Something might be useless, inefficient, and outdated, but anyone can avoid saying so outright by declaring it not fit for purpose.

O

on a journey

An annoying cliché much used to refer not to a trip or expedition, but to a process of development. There is nothing wrong with using the word journey metaphorically in this way, especially if the process of development is long and difficult, but the expression has become annoying because it is so overused in trivial contexts, especially on television shows, as in *All the finalists have improved immensely since the start of the show. They have been on a journey.*

the one and only

An irritating phrase used to introduce or describe someone, such as an entertainer, to emphasize how good they are and what a unique talent they have, as in *It is my pleasure to introduce the one and only Merlin the Magician.* Since every human being is unique and therefore can be described as the **one and only**, the cliché is pretty meaningless.

one for the road

An outdated cliché that is used to refer to a last drink before people set off for home, as in *It's nearly closing time. Let's have one for the road*. Nowadays when there is a clampdown on drink-driving to avoid accidents and death on the roads it is a cliché that should not be acted on unless the drinker is on foot.

one hundred and ten percent

A modern cliché which emphasizes the enormous amount of effort that is expended on something, as in *Management expects one hundred and ten per cent from all its sales staff all the time.* Many people find the cliché annoying because it refers to a mathematical impossibility, the maximum percentage being one hundred percent. Others object to it because it reflects a culture that expects workers to spend too much time at their employment, leaving not enough with their families.

one over the eight

A cliché which refers to the fact that someone has consumed

too much alcohol and is far from sober, as in *I saw Tom staggering down the road last night. He had obviously had one over the eight.* The cliché was originally found in services' slang when a total of eight beers was apparently considered to be the amount that was safe for a man to drink before he was likely to become drunk and incapable. This amount would horrify doctors nowadays when they are always trying to get men to stick to a limit of 21 units of alcohol a week and women to 14 units.

only time will tell

A cliché suggesting that the outcome of something is unlikely to be known for a considerable time, but it is often used by people, for example by television reporters, to bring a report or story to an end when they cannot think of anything else to say, as in *Will they ever find out what exactly happened here? Only time will tell.* A more formal version of the cliché is **time alone will tell**.

only too pleased

A deceptive cliché in that it sounds as though the person

using it is very happy to do something, usually to help, although this is sometimes not the case: the cliché is often used simply as a polite convention and the person using it may be anything other than glad, but may be obliged to pretend to be happy, perhaps to please a customer, as in *I'll be only too pleased to carry all your packages to your car for you, madam.*

on this auspicious occasion

An annoying and pompous cliché used with the intention of making a speech or introduction sound more impressive. The word **auspicious** means indicating that something is likely to be successful, but the cliché is frequently used to indicate that the occasion referred to is simply a particularly important one, although this may not even be the case, as in *This is our annual dinner and we are fortunate enough to have persuaded the mayor to say a few words on this auspicious occasion.*

opening gambit

A cliché used to refer to something that someone says or

does at the beginning of a discussion or situation, often one that they hope will bring them some form of early advantage, as in *I had hoped to ask for a salary increase, but the boss's opening gambit was that there was to be a pay freeze starting immediately*. The word **opening** is really redundant as the word **gambit** on its own refers to an opening. The cliché is particularly common in journalese. A **gambit** is an opening move in chess.

open the floodgates

A cliché referring to the removal of some form of restriction or control so that an overwhelming amount or number of something is released. The cliché is common in journalese where it is often an exaggeration. It is also common among politicians and other people in authority who use it as an excuse for not removing some form of restriction, whether or not this is likely to result in overwhelming amounts or numbers, as in *If we allow one pupil to leave school before the end of the school year to take up a job, it will open the floodgates.*

out of sight, out of mind *see* **absence makes the heart**

grow fonder *(p.8)*

outside your comfort zone

A cliché used to indicate that you are in a situation in which you do not feel comfortable, confident or secure, as in *I felt a bit outside my comfort zone at the conference. It was a bit high-powered for my liking.* Often a simple word such as 'uncomfortable' will do just as well as this rather high-flown cliché. The cliché is often used as part of business jargon to encourage people to be more ambitious and to expand their horizons, as in *It is our aim to encourage office staff to step outside their comfort zones and train for management posts.*

an own goal

An expression meaning that something someone does is harmful or disadvantageous to their own interests, as in *It was an own goal on the part of the young woman when she sold the story of her affair with the MP to a tabloid. The newspaper also revealed unsavoury details of her own past, including several extra-marital affairs.* If you bring about an own goal you are said to **score an own goal**, also a cliché. The expression has its origins in football where it describes the kicking of a ball between the goalposts on your own team's side of the field.

P

pale into insignificance

A cliché which sounds formal and literary, but it has become a fixed expression which is commonly used today. It is used to indicate that something which may seem very bad, serious, important, large etc when considered on its own, seems much less so when compared with something worse, more serious, more important, larger etc, as in *The amount of money spent on government grants to charities pales into insignificance when compared with that spent on defence.*

par for the course

A cliché meaning just what you might expect, especially when what is expected is not good, as in *The train's late again, but that's par for the course on this line.* The expression has a sporting background, having its origins in the game of golf where the word par is used to refer to the number of strokes considered standard for a particular hole.

parlous *see* **in a parlous state** *(p.61)*

past the/its sell-by date

A cliché derived from the fact that perishable foodstuffs have to be stamped with the date which they should be sold by in order to be at their best. The food use dates from the later part of the twentieth century and the expression quickly spread to people, being used to refer to someone who is no longer considered to be useful or effective, as in *When we take over the company we'll probably keep on most of the younger staff, but we'll get rid of those that are past their sell-by date.* It can be annoyingly ageist and insulting, but it is sometimes nowadays used in a humorous or ironic context, as in *I'm just over 30 and when I go to that club I feel that I'm past my sell-by date!*

past *see* **put the past behind you** *(p.103)*

the patter of tiny feet

An old-fashioned sounding cliché dating from the late nineteenth century which many people find too coy or twee for the modern taste. The expression sometimes refers to the presence of children, but, more often, is used to refer to the fact that a baby is expected, as in *I hear that you and your husband are looking forward to hearing the patter of tiny feet.* The modern tendency is to speak more frankly about pregnancy.

pew *see* **take a pew** *(p.118)*

proactive

An annoying cliché which is widely used, particularly in a work environment. It is supposed to be used to refer to someone who is the opposite of **reactive**. A reactive person or group takes action in response to something that has happened. A proactive person takes action in advance. The cliché is much admired by people placing job advertisements, as in *We are seeking a proactive and dynamic leader for our sales force.* Frequently now, the word is used by people who think it sounds impressive, but do not really know what it means, and use it virtually as a synonym for **active**.

pull yourself together

A brusque cliché which is bound to irritate and upset someone who is on the receiving end of it when they are miserable or depressed. If you are emotionally falling apart and hardly have the energy to crawl out from under the duvet, this is the last piece of advice that you will find helpful. It is often meted out by someone who usually keeps their own emotions at bay and prides themselves on keeping a stiff upper lip.

purpose *see* **not fit for purpose** *(p.91)*

push the envelope

A modern cliché meaning to take a risk, to try to go beyond what are thought to be the limits, boundaries or limitations, as in *When it comes to introducing violent, grotesque death in films this director certainly pushes the envelope.* Annoyingly, many people use this cliché without knowing its meaning or the contexts in which it can be used, but they think it sounds voguish and impressive. In origin the expression is thought to refer not to an envelope in the stationery sense, but to the limitations of speed and other specifications which dictate the performance of an aircraft. Although the figurative expression did not become popular until the late twentieth century, the aviation meaning of to make an aircraft go beyond its known performance limits in order to establish its exact capabilities dates from the 1940s.

put the past behind you

One of several annoying clichés used to people who are experiencing some kind of misfortune. Many people cannot think of what to say in such situations but they would be as well saying nothing and offering practical help, instead of turning to clichés. **Put the past behind you** is meant to encourage the person to forget the misfortune and plan for the future, but it is likely to upset and annoy anyone who feels unable to do so. Besides, the expression sounds ludicrous. The past is behind us whether we like it or not.

Q

quality time

A cliché used to refer to leisure time that a person passes with their children, partner etc, especially when they are spending a long time at work, as in *She tries to get away from the office in time to spend an hour's quality time with her two children before they go to bed.* The suggestion is that the quality of this time makes up for the lack of quantity, but many people find the cliché annoying and think that it simply masks a guilt complex about not spending much time with the family. It is one of many expressions that came to Britain from America and became very popular in the 1980s.

quantum leap

An expression which many people find annoying because it is not only overused but it is also often used inappropriately of quite minor transitions, as in *Our child is taking the quantum leap from playgroup to nursery school.* People often use it to make what they have to say sound more impressive, often not knowing what the expression means. The cliché has a scientific background and originates from nuclear physics where a quantum leap is a sudden transition from one energy state to another within the submicroscopic atom.

quite frankly

A phrase sometimes used as an indication that the person employing it is speaking exceptionally bluntly, as in *Quite frankly, I no longer care what happens to him*. However, it is often used virtually meaninglessly as a filler by people for whom it has become an annoying habit. Sometimes the **quite** is omitted and the cliché becomes just **frankly**. A famous use of this occurs in the last scene of the film *Gone with the Wind* (1939) when Rhett Butler says to Scarlett O'Hara 'Frankly, my dear, I don't give a damn.'

a race against time

A dramatic-sounding cliché used to suggest an extremely urgent situation, as in *The injured climber needs immediate surgery in order to save his leg. It's going to be a race against time to get him to hospital.* Annoyingly, the level of urgency is often exaggerated and the cliché is much overused, especially in journalese.

the ravages of time

A cliché which sounds rather literary and archaic. However, it is still quite commonly used because it has become a fixed phrase and people tend not to think about the individual words that make it up when they use it. The cliché refers to the damage and destruction that the passage of time causes, as in *The village had been abandoned by the islanders long ago and it had virtually been obliterated by the ravages of time.* Nowadays, it is sometimes used humorously to refer to the human body or complexion, as in *I'm going to a formal dinner tonight. I'd better get out my make-up bag and try to repair the ravages of time.*

a reality check

A modern cliché which is American in origin and which is used to remind someone that they must be realistic and look at the facts of a situation instead of having unrealistic or unreasonable expectations, as in *The teenagers are planning to get married and think that two can live as cheaply as one. They need a reality check.* The cliché can be extremely annoying when it is overused and when it implies that the only realistic way of looking at things is that of the person using the cliché.

relationship *see* in a relationship *(p.62)*

the rest is history

A remark used to indicate that no more need be said about something because the rest is already well-known to your listeners, as in *She submitted a short story to a magazine, won first prize, had it published in an anthology, was given a book deal by the publisher and the rest is history.* The cliché is often overused in journalese and it can be annoying if you, in fact, do not know the rest of the details.

result *see* **get a result** *(p.47)*

return to the fray

A cliché which sounds rather literary and archaic, but is still quite commonly used simply because it has become a fixed phrase and people tend not to think about its meaning. The cliché means to take up some form of work or activity that you have set aside for some reason. The word **fray** is an archaic word meaning affray or conflict and, although the cliché sometimes refers to a scene of conflict, as in *The committee has been meeting all morning without coming to a decision and so we have to return to the fray after lunch,* this is not necessarily the case, as in *I'm having a marvellous holiday and I'm certainly not looking forward to returning to the fray on Monday.*

rock *see* **between a rock and a hard place** *(p.19)*

rocket *see* **it's not rocket science** *(p.69)*

S

a safe pair of hands

A cliché, common in political circles and the business world, used to refer to someone who is thought to be reliable and competent and unlikely to make any major errors. However, the expression often also carries the suggestion that the person referred to is unimaginative and dull, as in *The new minister is a safe pair of hands. He'll keep the department steady until the election in a few months time. Then there's likely to be a change.* The cliché can be irritating, especially as **the safe pair of hands** often does not live up to its reputation. The origin of the phrase lies in cricket where it refers to someone who can be relied upon not to drop the ball or miss a catch.

sales call *see* **this is not a sales call** *(p.122)*

same *see* **by the same token** *(p.22)*

same old, same old

A modern cliché used in informal contexts to emphasize that there is nothing new, unusual or exciting going on, the suggestion being that life is fairly boring as in *'What did you do today?' 'Same old, same old. I was studying. My exams are next week.'* The cliché is in line with a recent trend to use short forms of phrases that are already quite short, a trend that older people especially find annoying and rather sloppy. This one is short for something like **same old thing** or **same old story**. Sometimes the phrase is not repeated and is just **same old**.

the school of hard knocks

A cliché referring to experience of life, often with accompanying hardship, in contrast to formal further education. It is often used rather smugly and annoyingly by people who have made a lot of money, or have otherwise been successful, although they did not stay on at school or go to college or university, as in *My parents were far too poor to send me to college. I was educated at the school of hard knocks, but I'm now a millionaire several times over.* The suggestion behind the expression is that people who do experience the benefits of further education have a much softer life. The same idea is expressed by the **university of life**, as in *I was educated at the university of life and I now own three companies. Yet half of these students never do anything with their lives, for all their expensive education.*

score an own goal *see* **an own goal** *(p.97)*

seminal

A word that is a source of annoyance because it is overused and used in inappropriate contexts often by people who wrongly think that it makes what they have to say more impressive and who might not know exactly what it means. It means very important and having a great influence on later developments, as in *He is famous for his seminal work on transplant surgery.* It should not be used of minor or trivial things.

a slight technical hitch

An ambiguous cliché acting as a standard excuse and

offered as part of an apology, for example, for the delay or cancellation of a transport service or the breakdown of a machine, as in *We apologize for the late-running service to London Waterloo. This is due to a slight technical hitch.* This cliché tends to annoy people rather than placate them as it offers no specific reason for what has gone wrong and people like to have a bit more information when they have been inconvenienced. Companies have become more inventive, although not necessarily more informative, when offering excuses. Thus, railway companies have been known to suggest that delayed trains were a result of the wrong kind of snow on the line. *See* **due to circumstances beyond our control** *(p.34)*.

soon as

A cliché which is in line with a recent trend to use short forms of phrases that are already quite short, a trend that older people especially find annoying and rather sloppy. This one is short for **as soon as possible** and it sounds abrupt and much ruder than the full version or even than the abbreviation **ASAP**, as in *You're late. Get here soon as!*

space *see* **I need some space** *(p.63)*

speculation is/was rife

A journalists' favourite, this cliché indicates that many people are forming opinions about something without knowing all the facts, as in *Police have not released the name of the man they have arrested in connection with the murder, but speculation is rife in the village.* **Rife** is an adjective indicating that something is widespread and it is usually associated with something bad or unpleasant, as in *Poverty and disease are rife in the area.* The cliché, in common with some other clichés, sounds quite formal and old-fashioned to be still relatively common today, but it has become a fixed phrase and people use it without thinking about the individual words.

speed *see* **up to speed** *(p.128)*

spend more time with the/his/her/my family

This euphemistic phrase is well used in business and political fields as a reason for someone leaving an important job. The resignation is usually a result of a misdemeanour that made it impossible for the person to stay in the job and often the only alternative to resignation is the sack, as in *The minister has announced that he is resigning from his cabinet post to spend more time with his family*. The expression was popularized by politicians in the 1980s and is particularly annoying because it suggests that the person resigning does so for the best of reasons instead of the worst.

star-studded

A cliché often applied to the cast of a performance of some kind, implying that the members of this cast are all very well-known and exceptionally talented. The expression is a favourite with publicity people whose task is to promote the show, but it is frequently a decidedly exaggerated way of describing the cast, some of whom may be little-known and some unheard of, as is common with many so-called celebs these day.

the straight and narrow

A cliché used to refer to a law-abiding or virtuous way of life, as in *The police have let you off with a caution this time but, from now on, you'll have to stick to the straight and narrow*. Often the phrase is used humorously nowadays, as in *I'm not straying from the straight and narrow on my stag night. My wife-to-be would kill me if I got drunk and incapable.* It is a fixed phrase and few people think about its origin which is biblical, being a reference to a passage from Matthew 7:14, 'Strait is the gate, and narrow is the way, which leadeth unto life, and few there be that find it.'

stuff happens *see* **these things happen** *(p.121)*

swingeing cuts

A cliché referring to severe budget reductions, as in *We will have to make swingeing cuts in our production and distribution costs if the firm is going to survive.* We are particularly familiar with this expression during times of economic recession because it is a great favourite with journalists and commentators. **Swingeing** is a word that is liable to cause problems because it is apt to be spelt wrongly as *swinging* and pronounced wrongly to rhyme with *swinging* instead of *bingeing*.

sword *see* **fall on your sword** *(p.40)*

syndrome

A cliché which is found particularly annoying by those who are aware of its origin and regard the modern use as a misuse. As a modern cliché it is usually applied to a set of actions, opinions, attitudes etc that is typical of a particular type of person, attitude, problem etc, as in *She suffers from the poor little rich girl syndrome.* In origin, it is one of those expressions that have a technical background, in this case medical, but have become used more generally. The medical term refers to a set of symptoms that together make up a known medical condition, as in *The child has been diagnosed with Down's syndrome.*

T

take a pew

An expression which is the nearest many people ever get to a church these days, the word **pew** being used to refer to a long wooden seat in a church where members of the congregation sit. The informal expression, however, refers to any seat, take a pew being an invitation to sit down on whatever seat is available, as in *I'm sorry to have kept you waiting. Take a pew.*

take it from me

One of those clichés that do not mean what they say. The wording suggests that the speaker is giving or handing something to someone. Instead, the cliché is simply being used to introduce a comment or opinion. It is sometimes used to emphasize the truth of this comment, but it is often uttered by someone for whom it has become an annoying habit, as in *Take it from me. Her husband will turn out to be the murderer.*

team player

A cliché with its origins in sport, but mostly used in a business context to refer to someone who works well as part of a team. It is a favourite with people drawing up job advertisements, as in *The successful candidate will have a proven track record in sales and marketing and recognize the importance of being a team player.*

technical *see* **a slight technical hitch** *(p.112)*

tell me about it!

A modern cliché used in informal contexts to emphasize how much you agree with what has just been said, as in *'Rents of flats round here are pretty expensive.' 'Tell me about it! I've given up trying to find a flat I can afford. I'm going to have to stay at home with my parents.'* An older cliché expressing the same sentiment is **you're telling me**!

territory *see* **it goes with the territory** *(p.66)*

that's life

One of several remarks that reflect a resigned attitude to life and indicate that some disappointment or misfortune in life is inevitable. People use it to friends and acquaintances who have experienced such disappointment or misfortune, as in *It's too bad that you didn't get the job you applied for, but that's life!* As is the case with other clichés of this kind, people on the receiving end often find it very annoying. Such platitudes bring no comfort whatsoever.

there are thousands worse off than you

A cliché which is used to remind a person who has just suffered from misfortune that their condition is much less serious than that of many others in the world, as in *It's too bad that you've lost your job and that you're going to have to sell your flat, but there are thousands worse off than you. A lot of the people made redundant have families to support.* This is more likely to upset and annoy the sufferer rather than comfort them. Their misfortune may be trivial when taken in a world context, but to them it is all-consuming.

there you go

A phrase which is used meaninglessly as a filler, often when someone, such as a shop assistant, is giving someone something, as in *There you go, Mrs Jones. Half a dozen cakes. That'll be three pounds sixty, please.* Like most meaningless clichés, this is a source of irritation to some people.

these things happen

A cliché that is often used to remind those suffering from some misfortune that they are far from being unique and that bad things happen to people all the time, as in *It's terrible that your husband has gone off with his secretary, but these things happen.* For some reason it is common for people to respond to other people's misfortune with such unhelpful and annoying clichés when what these people are seeking is some sympathy. A more modern version of this is **stuff happens** and a cruder version is **shit happens**. *See* **there are thousands worse than you** *(p.120).*

the thing is

One of those clichés that do not add any meaning to

what is being said, but are used as a filler by those for whom it has become an annoying habit. The cliché is sometimes used to introduce some kind of explanation or excuse, as in *I'm thinking of leaving my job. The thing is I've got very bored with it.*

think of the thousands of children starving in Africa

A cliché, with various alternative forms of wording, used by desperate parents trying to get their offspring to eat something at meal times. This rarely works as the children are either too young to understand, do not really care about the fate of children far away when they are being forced to eat food which they do not want, or say that they do not mind if the food being offered is sent to the starving children.

this is not a sales call

A cliché used by people trying to engage your attention on some commercial venture at the most inconvenient part of your day, when you are trying to cook the evening meal and do several other things at once. People have long since tired of sales calls and either do not answer the phone at that time or put the phone down immediately that they realize that someone is trying to sell them a new kitchen, car insurance, cheaper phone rates, a unique holiday deal etc. This cliché is often meant to be a cunning ruse to avoid such actions, but few people are fooled by it and, indeed, it can arouse more annoyance than a direct sales pitch.

time alone will tell *see* **only time will tell** *(p.94)*

to be honest

A cliché which sounds as though the person using it is doing so to emphasize the truth of what they are saying, as though the listener were likely to query this. This is not usually the case. The cliché is often used meaninglessly just as a filler by people for whom it has become an annoying habit. *See* **in all honesty** *(p.61)*.

to coin a phrase *see* **coin a phrase** *(p.27)*

tomorrow is another day

One of several clichés which are annoying because they state the obvious. No one is likely to need telling that tomorrow is another day. Of course, the expression is not just used to remind people of the existence of tomorrow, but to emphasize that tomorrow might well bring new opportunities or that anything not finished or accomplished today might be tackled tomorrow. The expression was popularized by the last words of the film *Gone with the Wind* (1939), based on the novel by Margaret Mitchell. Scarlett O'Hara closes the film with the lines *I'll go home and I'll think of some way to get him back. After all, tomorrow is another day.*

too close to call

A cliché that almost always appears at times of political elections. It is supposed to be used in situations in which the outcome is very difficult to predict because the various opinion polls suggest that two or more candidates have much the same level of support, as in *We don't yet know who will be MP for this area. The election is next week and the likely result is still too close to call.* However, it seems to be a cliché that journalists cannot resist and it is sometimes annoyingly used simply to increase interest in the election on the grounds that one where the result is unpredictable is more likely to be exciting. This is felt necessary as political elections these days seem to arouse more apathy than interest.

too little too late

A cliché which is much used in relation to politics, and often with a reference to money or resources, as in *Organizations representing the homeless say the funding that has just been assigned to them by the government is too little too late.* The cliché is now well-worn, mostly because the concept is true of so many situations.

too much information!

A modern cliché used to try to prevent someone from going on giving intimate or personal details which might embarrass the hearer, as in *Too much information! We don't want to hear about your lover's exploits.*

too numerous to mention

A cliché that is sometimes used to mean what it says, namely that there are too many people or things to name them individually. However, annoyingly, it is sometimes used by public speakers to introduce a list of the very people or things that are supposed to be too numerous to mention. The phrase sounds rather formal but it has become a fixed expression which people use without thinking of the meaning.

trouble

see **asking for trouble/it** *(p.12)*
see **get into trouble** *(p.48)*

U

unaccustomed as I am to public speaking...

A pompous and irritating cliché that is, fortunately, now often used in a humorous way by people who are poking fun at the phrase. Formerly, the cliché was (and still is occasionally) used by public speakers, such as after-dinner speakers, who felt that it made them sound more impressive, as in *Unaccustomed as I am to public speaking, I would like to welcome to you all to our annual dinner and to express the hope that you all have an enjoyable time*. Winston Churchill used the expression in his first political speech in 1897, referring to the expression as 'the well-worn and time-honoured apology'.

the university of life *see* **the school of hard knocks** *(p.111)*

an unmitigated disaster

A cliché used to refer to something that is considered a

complete failure, as in *It was a very wet day and hardly anyone came to the outdoor concert. Financially, it was an unmitigated disaster.* The expression sounds very formal, but it is quite commonly used. Indeed, it is often over-used as it tends to exaggerate the extent of the failure of a situation.

unsung hero

A cliché used to refer to someone who has done something particularly brave, but has not received any official or public recognition of this, as in *These young soldiers were the unsung heroes of the war.* Ancient writers wrote classical epics or songs about the heroes of the day and those who did not feature in these were literally 'unsung'. The cliché sounds very literary, but it is still commonly used today, particularly in journalese.

up to speed

A cliché meaning having all the latest information concerning something, as in *I need you all to be up to speed on the sales campaign by this afternoon's meeting.* Literally meaning operating at the required rate, the cliché is widely used in business contexts, often by people for whom the phrase has become an irritating habit.

user-friendly

A cliché used to describe something that is supposedly relatively easy to operate or understand, as in *Each machine comes with a user-friendly instruction manual*. The problem is that the person who has used the cliché often overestimates the ability or understanding of the person who is going to do the using so that many people find the cliché inappropriate and annoying, as in *The instructions with this flat-pack furniture claim to be user-friendly, but I don't understand a word of them.*

the usual suspects

A cliché used to describe the people who are usually involved with something, as in *'Were there a lot of people at the protest meeting?' 'No, not really. Just the usual suspects.'* The expression was originally used in connection with police work, **the usual suspects** being those criminals whom the police think are most likely to have been involved in a crime. The phrase was used in this connection in the film *Casablanca* (1942), but it was the film entitled *The Usual Suspects* (1995) that really popularized the expression and it is now used as a cliché in a wide range of situations.

valued customer

A cliché not often used, as it suggests, to refer to a customer who is particularly appreciated by a business firm. Rather, it is an annoying commercial cliché used in promotional material and campaigns to try to get a customer to buy even more and so spend more money, as in *As a valued customer, you have been sent an advance copy of our Christmas catalogue so that you can make your purchases in plenty of time* and *As a valued customer, you are being offered the opportunity to increase the credit limit on your card.*

vexed question

A difficult issue or problem that is much discussed, but is very difficult to find a solution to, as in *The landlord says that we can move in next month, but there remains the vexed question of where we are going to find the deposit.* The cliché is sometimes used wrongly by people who think that **vexed** has the usual modern meaning of irritated or annoyed. In origin this cliché is a translation of the Latin phrase *quaestio vexata*.

wait and see

A cliché that is particularly annoying to people who are impatiently waiting for a reply or decision. It is frequently used by parents to children who find it even more irritating. If they're bursting with impatience to know what they've got as a birthday present they do not want to be told to wait and see. The phrase was a great favourite of Henry Asquith (1852-1928) when he was Prime Minister of Britain.

we'll see

Another cliché much used by parents to children and a source of great annoyance to the said children. Parents use the phrase to avoid having to reply to a request or demand from their offspring. Often their intention is to get the child home before saying no, so that the resultant tantrum can be carried out in the privacy of the home, as in *'Can I have one of those jumbo packs of sweets?' 'We'll see.'* Children have long ago realized the negative implications of **we'll see** and frequently have a public tantrum anyway. Of course, some conscientious parents really mean that they will give the matter consideration.

whatever

Originally known to most of us as a pronoun or as a determiner, as in *For whatever reason he has refused to attend,* the word is now in widespread use as a laconic reply, as in *'Would you like curry or pizza for dinner?' 'Whatever!'* Whether you regard this use as an annoying cliché or as a perfectly acceptable part of modern speech probably depends on your age. Older people tend to be irritated by the disregard or lack of interest that the word suggests.

what goes around comes around

A cliché, originating in America, which indicates that people will one day have to face the consequences of their actions, as in *Jack treated his parents very badly and now his children have grown up and are treating him in the same way. What goes around comes around.* The expression can apply to good things, but it mostly applies to bad things. The cliché is annoying in that it is over-optimistic. Unfortunately, by no means does everyone have to face the consequences of their bad or wrong actions.

when all is said and done

A cliché which is sometimes used to refer to the most important point of a situation, as in *The young couple discuss endlessly what house is right for them, but, when all is said and done, they will have to settle for what they can afford*. Often, however, the cliché does not add anything to the meaning of what is being said. People use it is a filler, often to play for time when they are thinking of something to say, for example when being asked a question on television or radio. It is also used by people who think, quite wrongly, that such phrases make what they are saying sound more impressive. It is used in the same way as **at the end of the day** *(p.13)* and **in the final analysis** *(p.64)*.

a window

This cliché refers to a time, usually a period of limited

duration, when there is an opportunity to do something, as in, *We need dry weather to get the harvest in and, according to the weather forecasters, we're likely to get a window early next week.* The expression is so overused that it has become a cliché and people frequently use it rather pompously of their appointment diaries, as in *I have a window tomorrow afternoon at four o'clock if you can come to my office then.* A longer form of the expression is **a window of opportunity**. The cliché has its origins in the US space programme in the 1960s when a launch window referred to the time during which a rocket had to be launched if it was to get into the correct orbit.

win the hearts and minds of

A cliché meaning to persuade a group of people to offer support emotionally and intellectually and not just physically. The expression has a military background since it was stated as one of the aims of the Americans during the Vietnam war. It was used by them again with relevance to the Iraqis when America, Britain and their allies invaded Iraq. The expression was disliked by many, being seen as a cover-up for what was considered by many people as an illegal invasion. However, the cliché remained popular in journalese and began to be used more generally, especially in politics, as in *Our party must win the hearts and minds of the electorate if we are going to get into power again.*

with all due respect

A cliché which irritates people because the person using the expression as an introduction to a comment rarely means it. Indeed, it is often used to introduce some kind of criticism or insult, as in *With all due respect, I think you enjoy interfering in their lives.*

wrong *see* get out of bed on the wrong side *(p.48)*

Y

a yawning gap

A cliché much used to emphasize how far apart things are, as in *There is still a yawning gap between the cost of the project and what we have managed to raise so far.* The phrase is particularly common in journalese and is frequently used as an exaggeration.

... years young

A cliché used instead of **... years old** which is, of course, the correct convention. Like **the young of all ages**, the cliché is used supposedly to make the older or elderly members of a group feel younger, but simply makes most of them feel patronized. It is frequently used by someone addressing a group or by journalists, radio presenters etc, as in *Special birthday wishes go to Mrs Margaret Jones who is 90 years young today.*

you know what I mean

One of those annoying clichés that rarely add any meaning to what is being said, but have become an annoying habit with some people. Some attach it to just about any statement, however irrelevant this is, as in *Have you not met the new manager? I can't stand him. You know what I mean.*

you know what I think?

A cliché in the form of a seeming question that is not really seeking a reply. The person using the cliché does not really want to know if the listener knows their thoughts without being told. It is one of those annoying clichés that rarely add any meaning to what is being said, but are used as a filler by people for whom the cliché has become an annoying habit, as in *You know what I think? I think he's lying.* At best, it is used to add emphasis to what is being said. **Do you know what I think?** or **know what I think?** are alternative forms of the cliché.

the young of all ages

A cliché that is presumably meant to make the older or

elderly members of a group feel young in all but years, but it simply makes many of them feel patronized. It is often used by someone making a speech, often one with a ring of forced jollity and pompousness about it, or in some form of promotional material designed to encourage as many people as possible to attend a performance or to purchase some form of merchandise, as in *The pantomime is likely to appeal to the young of all ages.* An alternative form of the cliché is **children of all ages**.

your call is important to us

An extremely irritating cliché that is encountered by most of us many times when dealing with our business affairs. Such affairs are, of course, often conducted by telephone and require a great deal of button-pushing before we are eventually put on hold. Then comes a series of comments presumably aimed at defusing our impatience, but actually serving only to inflame it. Of these comments **your call is important to us** is one of the most annoying as it is clearly untrue. If our call were really important to them wouldn't they employ more people to answer the phone?!

you're telling me! *see* **tell me about it!** *(p.119)*

The World's Funniest Proverbs

JAMES ALEXANDER

Beauty is in the eye of the beer holder

Don't take life too seriously - it's not permanent

Multi-tasking: the art of screwing up everything all at once

Never marry for money; you will borrow cheaper

ISBN 13: 978-1-906051-07-5,

HARDBACK, £5.99

The World's Funniest Puns

Archaeologist:
A man whose career
lies in ruins.

What's the
definition of
a will?
A dead giveaway.

Did you hear about
the butcher who
backed into a
meat grinder?
He got a little
behind in his work.

JAMES ALEXANDER

ISBN 13: 978-1-905102-66-2,
ISBN 10: 1-905102-66-6,
PAPERBACK, £4.99

www.crombiejardine.com